Clement of Alexandria

The Fragments

Clement of Alexandria
The Fragments

Clement of Alexandria
The Fragments

Published by
Lighthouse Christian Publishing
SAN 257-4330
5531 Dufferin Drive
Savage, Minnesota, 55378
United States of America

www.lighthousechristianpublishing.com

Introductory Note on Clement of Alexandria

[a.d. 153–193–217.] The second century of illumination is drawing to a close, as the great name of this Father comes into view, and introduces us to a new stage of the Church's progress. From Britain to the Ganges it had already made its mark. In all its Oriental identity, we have found it vigorous in Gaul and penetrating to other regions of the West. From its primitive base on the Orontes, it has extended itself to the deltas of the Nile; and the Alexandria of Apollos and of St. Mark has become the earliest seat of Christian learning. There, already, have the catechetical schools gathered the finest intellectual trophies of the Cross; and under the aliment of its library springs up something like a Christian university. Pantænus, "the Sicilian bee" from the flowery fields of Enna, comes to frame it by his industry, and store it with the sweets of his eloquence and wisdom. Clement, who had followed Tatian to the East, tracks Pantænus to Egypt, and comes with his Attic scholarship to be his pupil in the school of Christ. After Justin and Irenæus, he is to be reckoned the founder of Christian literature; and it is noteworthy how sublimely he begins to treat Paganism as a creed outworn, to be dismissed with contempt, rather than seriously wrestled with any longer.

His merciless exposure of the entire system of "lords many and gods many," seems to us, indeed, unnecessarily offensive. Why not spare us such details? But let us reflect, that, if such are our Christian instincts of delicacy, we owe it to this great reformer in no small proportion. For not content to show the Pagans that the very atmosphere was polluted by their mythologies, so that Christians, turn which way they would, must encounter pestilence, he becomes the ethical philosopher of Christians; and while he proceeds to dictate, even in minute details, the transformations to which the faithful must subject themselves in order "to escape the pollutions of the world," he sketches in outline the reformations which the Gospel imposes on society, and which nothing but the Gospel has ever enabled mankind to realize. "For with a celerity unsurpassable, and a benevolence to which we have ready access," says Clement, "the Divine Power hath filled the universe with the seed of salvation." Socrates and Plato had talked sublimely four hundred years before; but Lust and Murder were yet the gods of Greece, and men and women were like what they worshipped. Clement had been their disciple; but now, as the disciple of Christ, he was to exert a power over men and manners, of which they never dreamed.

Alexandria becomes the brain of Christendom: its heart was yet beating at Antioch, but the West was still receptive only, its hands and arms stretched forth towards the sunrise for further enlightenment. From the East it had obtained the Scriptures and their authentication, and from the same source was deriving the canons, the liturgies, and the creed of Christendom. The universal language of Christians is Greek. To a pagan emperor who had outgrown the ideas of Nero's time, it was no longer Judaism; but it was not less an Oriental superstition, essentially Greek in its features and its dress. "All the churches of the West," says the historian of Latin Christianity, "were Greek religious colonies. Their language was Greek, their organization Greek, their writers Greek, their Scriptures and their ritual were Greek. Through Greek, the communications of the churches of the West were constantly kept up with the East. . . . Thus the Church at Rome was but one of a confederation of Greek religious republics founded by Christianity." Now this confederation was the Holy Catholic Church.

Every Christian must recognize the career of Alexander, and the history of his empire, as an immediate precursor of the Gospel. The patronage of letters by the Ptolemies at Alexandria, the translation of the Hebrew Scriptures into the dialect of the Hellenes, the creation of a new terminology in the language of the Greeks, by which ideas of faith and of truth might find access to the mind of a heathen world,—these were preliminaries to the preaching of the Gospel to mankind, and to the composition of the New Testament of our Lord and Savior. He Himself had prophetically visited Egypt, and the idols were now to be removed before his presence. There a powerful Christian school was to make itself felt for ever in the definitions of orthodoxy; and in a new sense was that prophecy to be understood, "Out of Egypt have I called my Son."

The genius of Apollos was revived in his native city. A succession of doctors was there to arise, like him, "eloquent men, and mighty in the Scriptures." Clement tells us of his masters in Christ, and how, coming to Pantænus, his soul was filled with a deathless element of divine knowledge. He speaks of the apostolic tradition as received through his teachers hardly at second-hand. He met in that school, no doubt, some, at least, who recalled Ignatius and Polycarp; some, perhaps, who as children had heard St. John when he could only exhort his congregations to "love one another." He could afterwards speak of himself as in the next succession after the apostles.

He became the successor of Pantænus in the catechetical school, and had Origen for his pupil, with other eminent men. He was also ordained a presbyter. He seems to have compiled his *Stromata* in the reigns of Commodus and Severus. If, at this time, he was about forty years of age, as seems likely, we must conceive of his birth at Athens, while

Antoninus Pius was emperor, while Polycarp was yet living, and while Justin and Irenæus were in their prime.

Alexander, bishop of Jerusalem, speaks of Clement, in turn, as his master: "for we acknowledge as fathers those blessed saints who are gone before us, and *to whom we shall go after a little time* the truly blest Pantænus, I mean, and the holy Clemens, my teacher, who was to me so greatly useful and helpful." St. Cyril of Alexandria calls him "a man admirably learned and skilful, and one that searched to the depths all the learning of the Greeks, with an exactness rarely attained before." So Theodoret says, "He surpassed all others, and *was a holy man.*" St. Jerome pronounces him the most learned of all the ancients; while Eusebius testifies to his theological attainments, and applauds him as an "incomparable master of Christian philosophy." But the rest shall be narrated by our translator, Mr. Wilson.

The following is the original Introductory Notice:—

Titus Flavius Clemens, the illustrious head of the Catechetical School at Alexandria at the close of the second century, was originally a pagan philosopher. The date of his birth is unknown. It is also uncertain whether Alexandria or Athens was his birthplace.

On embracing Christianity, he eagerly sought the instructions of its most eminent teachers; for this purpose travelling extensively over Greece, Italy, Egypt, Palestine, and other regions of the East. Only one of these teachers (who, from a reference in the *Stromata*, all appear to have been alive when he wrote) can be with certainty identified, viz., Pantænus, of whom he speaks in terms of profound reverence, and whom he describes as the greatest of them all. Returning to Alexandria, he succeeded his master Pantænus in the catechetical school, probably on the latter departing on his missionary tour to the East, somewhere about a.d. 189. He was also made a presbyter of the Church, either then or somewhat later. He continued to teach with great distinction till a.d. 202, when the persecution under Severus compelled him to retire from Alexandria. In the beginning of the reign of Caracalla we find him at Jerusalem, even then a great resort of Christian, and especially clerical, pilgrims. We also hear of him travelling to Antioch, furnished with a letter of recommendation by Alexander, bishop of Jerusalem. The close of his career is covered with obscurity. He is supposed to have died about a.d. 220.

Among his pupils were his distinguished successor in the Alexandrian school, Origen, Alexander bishop of Jerusalem, and, according to Baronius, Combefisius, and Bull, also Hippolytus.

The above is positively the sum of what we know of Clement's history.

His three great works, *The Exhortation to the Heathen* (λόγος ὁ προτρεπτικὸς πρὸς Ἕλληνας), *The Instructor, or Pædagogus* (παιδαγωγός), *The Miscellanies*, or *Stromata* (Στρωματεῖς), are among the most valuable remains of Christian antiquity, and the largest that belong to that early period.

The Exhortation, the object of which is to win pagans to the Christian faith, contains a complete and withering exposure of the abominable licentiousness, the gross imposture and sordidness of paganism. With clearness and cogency of argument, great earnestness and eloquence, Clement sets forth in contrast the truth as taught in the inspired Scriptures, the true God, and especially the personal Christ, the living Word of God, the Savior of men. It is an elaborate and masterly work, rich in felicitous classical allusion and quotation, breathing throughout the spirit of philosophy and of the Gospel, and abounding in passages of power and beauty.

The *Pædagogus, or Instructor*, is addressed to those who have been rescued from the darkness and pollutions of heathenism, and is an exhibition of Christian morals and manners,—a guide for the formation and development of Christian character, and for living a Christian life. It consists of three books. It is the grand aim of the whole work to set before the converts Christ as the only Instructor, and to expound and enforce His precepts. In the first book Clement exhibits the person, the function, the means, methods, and ends of the Instructor, who is the Word and Son of God; and lovingly dwells on His benignity and philanthropy, His wisdom, faithfulness, and righteousness.

The second and third books lay down rules for the regulation of the Christian, in all the relations, circumstances, and actions of life, entering most minutely into the details of dress, eating, drinking, bathing, sleeping, etc. The delineation of a life in all respects agreeable to the Word, a truly Christian life, attempted here, may, now that the Gospel has transformed social and private life to the extent it has, appear unnecessary, or a proof of the influence of ascetic tendencies. But a code of Christian morals and manners (a sort of "whole duty of man" and manual of good breeding combined) was eminently needed by those whose habits and characters had been molded under the debasing and polluting influences of heathenism; and who were bound, and were aiming, to shape their lives according to the principles of the Gospel, in the midst of the all but incredible licentiousness and luxury by which society around was incurably tainted. The disclosures which Clement, with solemn sternness, and often with caustic wit, makes of the prevalent voluptuousness and vice, form a very valuable contribution to our knowledge of that period.

The full title of the *Stromata*, according to Eusebius and Photius, was Τίτου Φλαυίου Κλήμεντος τῶν κατὰ τὴν ἀληθῆ φιλοσοφίαν γνωστικῶν ὑπομνημάτων στρωματεῖς— "Titus Flavius Clement's miscellaneous collections of speculative (gnostic) notes bearing upon the true philosophy." The aim of the work, in accordance with this title, is, in opposition to Gnosticism, to furnish the materials for the construction of a true gnosis, a Christian philosophy, on the basis of faith, and to lead on to this higher knowledge those who, by the discipline of the Pædagogus, had been trained for it. The work consisted originally of eight books. The eighth book is lost; that which appears under this name has plainly no connection with the rest of the *Stromata*. Various accounts have been given of the meaning of the distinctive word in the title (Στρωματεύς); but all agree in regarding it as indicating the miscellaneous character of its contents. And they are very miscellaneous. They consist of the speculations of Greek philosophers, of heretics, and of those who cultivated the true Christian gnosis, and of quotations from sacred Scripture. The latter he affirms to be the source from which the higher Christian knowledge is to be drawn; as it was that from which the germs of truth in Plato and the Hellenic philosophy were derived. He describes philosophy as a divinely ordered preparation of the Greeks for faith in Christ, as the law was for the Hebrews; and shows the necessity and value of literature and philosophic culture for the attainment of true Christian knowledge, in opposition to the numerous body among Christians who regarded learning as useless and dangerous. He proclaims himself an eclectic, believing in the existence of fragments of truth in all systems, which may be separated from error; but declaring that the truth can be found in unity and completeness only in Christ, as it was from Him that all its scattered germs originally proceeded. The *Stromata* are written carelessly, and even confusedly; but the work is one of prodigious learning, and supplies materials of the greatest value for understanding the various conflicting systems which Christianity had to combat.

It was regarded so much as the author's great work, that, on the testimony of Theodoret, Cassiodorus, and others, we learn that Clement received the appellation of Στρωματεύς (the Stromatist). In all probability, the first part of it was given to the world about a.d. 194. The latest date to which he brings down his chronology in the first book is the death of Commodus, which happened in a.d. 192; from which Eusebius9 concludes that he wrote this work during the reign of Severus, who ascended the imperial throne in a.d. 193, and reigned till a.d. 211. It is likely that the whole was composed ere Clement quitted Alexandria in a.d. 202. The publication of the *Pædagogus* preceded by a short time that of the *Stromata;* and the *Cohortatio* was written a short time before the *Pædagogus*, as is clear from statements made by Clement himself.

So multifarious is the erudition, so multitudinous are the quotations and the references to authors in all departments, and of all countries, the most of whose works have perished, that the works in question could only have been composed near an extensive library—hardly anywhere but in the vicinity of the famous library of Alexandria. They are a storehouse of curious ancient lore,—a museum of the fossil remains of the beauties and monstrosities of the world of pagan antiquity, during all the epochs and phases of its history. The three compositions are really parts of one whole. The central connecting idea is that of the Logos—the Word—the Son of God; whom in the first work he exhibits drawing men from the superstitions and corruptions of heathenism to faith; in the second, as training them by precepts and discipline; and in the last, as conducting them to that higher knowledge of the things of God, to which those only who devote themselves assiduously to spiritual, moral, and intellectual culture can attain. Ever before his eye is the grand form of the living personal Christ,—the Word, who "was with God, and who was God, but who became man, and dwelt among us."

Of course there is throughout plenty of false science, and frivolous and fanciful speculation.

Who is the rich man that shall be saved? (τίς ὁ σωζόμενος πλούσιος;) is the title of a practical treatise, in which Clement shows, in opposition to those who interpreted our Lord's words to the young ruler as requiring the renunciation of worldly goods, that the disposition of the soul is the great essential. Of other numerous works of Clement, of which only a few stray fragments have been preserved, the chief are the eight books of *The Hypotyposes*, which consisted of expositions of all the books of Scripture. Of these we have a few undoubted fragments. *The Adumbrations*, or *Commentaries on some of the Catholic Epistles*, and *The Selections from the Prophetic Scriptures*, are compositions of the same character, as far as we can judge, as *The Hypotyposes*, and are supposed by some to have formed part of that work.

Other lost works of Clement are:—

> The Treatise of Clement, the Stromatist, on the Prophet Amos.
> On Providence.
> Treatise on Easter.
> On Evil-speaking.
> Discussion on Fasting.
> Exhortation to Patience; or, To the newly baptized.
> Ecclesiastical Canon; or, Against the Judaizers.
> Different Terms.

The following are the names of treatises which Clement refers to as written or about to be written by him, but of which otherwise we have no trace or mention:—*On First Principles; On Prophecy; On the Allegorical Interpretation of Members and Affections when ascribed to God; On Angels; On the Devil; On the Origin of the Universe; On the Unity and Excellence of the Church; On the Offices of Bishops, Presbyters, Deacons, and Widows; On the Soul; On the Resurrection; On Marriage; On Continence; Against Heresies.*

Preserved among Clement's works is a fragment called *Epitomes of the Writings of Theodotus, and of the Eastern Doctrine*, most likely abridged extracts made by Clement for his own use, and giving considerable insight into Gnosticism.

Clement's quotations from Scripture are made from the Septuagint version, often inaccurately from memory, sometimes from a different text from what we possess, often with verbal adaptations; and not rarely different texts are blended together.

The works of Clement present considerable difficulties to the translator; and one of the chief is the state of the text, which greatly needs to be expurgated and amended. For this there are abundant materials, in the copious annotations and disquisitions, by various hands, collected together in Migne's edition; where, however, corruptions the most obvious have been allowed to remain in the text.

The publishers are indebted to Dr. W. L. Alexander for the poetical translations of the Hymns of Clement.

M. AURELIUS CASSIODORUS (WHOSE NAME IS ALSO SENATOR) WAS AN AUTHOR AND PUBLIC MAN OF THE SIXTH CENTURY, AND A VERY VOLUMINOUS WRITER. HE WOULD SHINE WITH A GREATER LUSTRE WERE HE NOT SO NEARLY LOST IN THE BRIGHTER LIGHT OF BOËTHIUS, HIS ILLUSTRIOUS CONTEMPORARY. AFTER THE DEATH OF HIS PATRON, THEODORIC, HE CONTINUED FOR A TIME IN THE PUBLIC SERVICE, AND IN HIGH POSITIONS, BUT, AT SEVENTY YEARS OF AGE, BEGAN ANOTHER CAREER, AND FOR TWENTY YEARS DEVOTED HIMSELF TO LETTERS AND THE PRACTICE OF PIETY IN A MONASTERY WHICH HE ESTABLISHED IN THE NEOPOLITAN KINGDOM, NEAR HIS NATIVE SQUILLACE. DIED ABOUT A.D. 560.] COMMENTS, I.E., *ADUMBRATIONES.* CASSIODORUS SAYS THAT HE HAD IN HIS TRANSLATION CORRECTED WHAT HE CONSIDERED ERRONEOUS IN THE ORIGINAL. SO FELL STATES: AND HE IS ALSO INCLINED TO BELIEVE THAT THESE FRAGMENTS ARE FROM CLEMENT'S LOST

WORK, THE ΎΠΟΤΥΠΏΣΕΙΣ, OF WHICH HE BELIEVES *THE*

ADUMBRATIONES OF CASSIODORUS TO BE A TRANSLATION.

FRAGMENTS OF CLEMENS ALEXANDRINUS.

I.—FROM THE LATIN TRANSLATION OF CASSIODORUS.

I.—COMMENTS ON THE FIRST EPISTLE OF PETER.

Chap. i. 3. "Blessed be the God and Father of our Lord Jesus Christ, who by His great mercy hath regenerated us." For if God generated us of matter, He afterwards, by progress in life, regenerated us.

"The Father of our Lord, by the resurrection of Jesus Christ:" who, according to your faith, rises again in us; as, on the other hand, He dies in us, through the operation of our unbelief. For He said again, that the soul never returns a second time to the body in this life; and that which has become angelic does not become unrighteous or evil, so as not to have the opportunity of again sinning by the assumption of flesh; but that in the resurrection the soul returns to the body, and both are joined to one another according to their peculiar nature, adapting themselves, through the composition of each, by a kind of congruity like a building of stones.

Besides, Peter says, "Ye also, as living stones, are built up a spiritual house;" meaning the place of the angelic abode, guarded in heaven. "For you," he says, "who are kept by the power of God, by faith and contemplation, to receive the end of your faith, the salvation of your souls."

Hence it appears that the soul is not naturally immortal; but is made immortal by the grace of God, through faith and righteousness, and by knowledge. "Of which salvation," he says, "the prophets have inquired and searched diligently," and what follows. It is declared by this that the prophets spake with wisdom, and that the Spirit of Christ was in them, according to the possession of Christ, and in subjection to Christ. For God works through archangels and kindred angels, who are called spirits of Christ.

"Which are now," he says, "reported unto you by them that have preached the Gospel unto you." The old things which were done by the prophets and escape the observation of most, are now revealed to you by the evangelists. "For to you," he says, "they are manifested by the Holy Ghost, who was sent;" that is the Paraclete, of whom the Lord said, "If I go not away, He will not come." "Unto whom," it is said, "the angels desire to look;" not the apostate angels, as most suspect, but, what is a divine truth, angels who desire to obtain the advantage of that perfection.

"By precious blood," he says, "as of a lamb without blemish and without spot." Here he touches on the ancient Levitical and sacerdotal celebrations; but means a soul pure through righteousness which is offered to God.

"Verily foreknown before the foundation of the world." Inasmuch as He was foreknown before every creature, because He was Christ. "But manifested in the last times" by the generation of a body. "Being born again, not of corruptible seed." The soul, then, which is produced along with the body is corruptible, as some think.

"But the word of the Lord," he says, "endureth for ever:" as well prophecy as divine doctrine.

"But ye are a chosen generation, a royal priesthood." That we are a chosen race by the election of God is abundantly clear. He says royal, because we are called to sovereignty and belong to Christ; and priesthood on account of the oblation which is made by prayers and instructions, by which are gained the souls which are offered to God.

"Who, when He was reviled," he says, "reviled not; when He suffered, threatened not." The Lord acted so in His goodness and patience. "But committed Himself to him that judged Him unrighteously:" whether Himself, so that, regarding Himself in this way, there is a transposition. He indeed gave Himself up to those who judged according to an unjust law; because He was unserviceable to them, inasmuch as He was righteous: or, He committed to God those who judged unrighteously, and without cause insisted on His death, so that they might be instructed by suffering punishment.

"For he that will love life, and see good days;" that is, who wishes to become eternal and immortal. And He calls the Lord life, and the days good, that is holy.

"For the eyes of the Lord," he says, "are upon the righteous, and His ears on their prayers:" he means the manifold inspection of the Holy Spirit. "The face of the Lord is on them that do evil;" that is, whether judgment, or vengeance, or manifestation.

"But sanctify the Lord Christ," he says, "in your hearts." For so you have in the Lord's prayer, "Hallowed be Thy name."

"For Christ," he says, "hath once suffered for our sins, the just for the unjust, that he might present us to God; being put to death in the flesh, but quickened in the spirit." He says these things, reducing them to their faith. That is, He became alive in our spirits.

"Coming," he says, "He preached to those who were once unbelieving." They saw not His form, but they heard His voice.

"When the long-suffering of God" holds out. God is so good, as to work the result by the teaching of salvation.

"By the resurrection," it is said, "of Jesus Christ:" that, namely, which is effected in us by faith.

"Angels being subjected to Him," which are the first order; and "principalities" being subject, who are of the second order; and "powers" being also subject, which are said to belong to the third order.

"Who shall give account," he says, "to Him who is ready to judge the quick and the dead."

These are trained through previous judgments. Therefore he adds, "For this cause was the Gospel preached also to the dead"—to us, namely, who were at one time unbelievers. "That they might be judged according to men," he says," in the flesh, but live according to God in the spirit."

Because, that is, they have fallen away from faith; whilst they are still in the flesh they are judged according to preceding judgments, that they might repent. Accordingly, he also adds, saying, "That they might live according to God in the spirit." So Paul also; for he, too, states something of this nature when he says, "Whom I have delivered to Satan, that he might live in the spirit;" that is, "as good stewards of the manifold grace of God." Similarly also Paul says, "Variously, and in many ways, God of old spake to our fathers."

"Rejoice," it is said, "that ye are partakers in the sufferings of Christ:" that is, if ye are righteous, ye suffer for righteousness' sake, as Christ suffered for righteousness. "Happy are ye, for the Spirit of God, who is the Spirit of His glory and virtue, resteth on you." This possessive "His" signifies also an angelic spirit: inasmuch as the glory of God those are, through whom, according to faith and righteousness, He is glorified, to honorable glory, according to the advancement of the saints who are brought in. "The Spirit of God on us," may be thus understood; that is, who through faith comes on the soul, like a gracefulness of mind and beauty of soul.

"Since," it is said, "it is time for judgment beginning at the house of God." For judgment will overtake these in the appointed persecutions.

"But the God of all grace," he says. "Of all grace," he says, because He is good, and the giver of all good things.

"Marcus, my son, saluteth you." Mark, the follower of Peter, while Peter publicly preached the Gospel at Rome before some of Cæsar's equites, and adduced many testimonies to Christ, in order that thereby they might be able to commit to memory what was spoken, of what was spoken by Peter, wrote entirely what is called the Gospel according to Mark. As Luke also may be recognized by the style, both to have composed the Acts of the Apostles, and to have translated Paul's Epistle to the Hebrews.

II.—COMMENTS ON THE EPISTLE OF JUDE.

Jude, who wrote the Catholic Epistle, the brother of the sons of Joseph, and very religious, whilst knowing the near relationship of the Lord, yet did not say that he himself was His brother. But what said he? "Jude, a servant of Jesus Christ,"—of Him as Lord; but "the brother of James." For this is true; he was His brother, (the son) of Joseph. "For certain men have entered unawares, ungodly men, who had been of old ordained and predestined to the judgment of our God;" not that they might become impious, but that, being now impious, they were ordained to judgment. "For the Lord God," he says, "who once delivered a people out of Egypt, afterward destroyed them that believed not;" that is, that He might train them through punishment. For they were indeed punished, and they perished on account of those that are saved, until they turn to the Lord. "But the angels," he says," that kept not their own pre-eminence," that, namely, which they received through advancement, "but left their own habitation," meaning, that is, the heaven and the stars, became, and are called apostates. "He hath reserved these to the judgment of the great day, in chains, under darkness." He means the place near the earth, that is, the dark air. Now he called "chains" the loss of the honor in which they had stood, and the lust of feeble things; since, bound by their own lust, they cannot be converted. "As Sodom and Gomorrah," he says.... By which the Lord signifies that pardon had been granted; and that on being disciplined they had repented. "Similarly to the same," he says, "also those dreamers,"—that is, who dream in their imagination lusts and wicked desires, regarding as good not that which is truly good, and superior to all good,—"defile the flesh, despise dominion, and speak evil of majesty," that is, the only Lord, who is truly our Lord, Jesus Christ, and alone worthy of praise. They "speak evil of majesty," that is, of the angels.

"When Michael, the archangel, disputing with the devil, debated about the body of Moses." Here he confirms the assumption of Moses. He is here called Michael, who through an angel near to us debated with the devil.

"But these," he says, "speak evil of those things which they know not; but what they know naturally, as brute beasts, in these things they corrupt themselves." He means that they eat, and drink, and indulge in uncleanness, and says that they do other things that are common to them with animals, devoid of reason.

"Woe unto them!" he says, "for they have gone in the way of Cain." For so also we lie under Adam's sin through similarity of sin. "Clouds," he says, "without water; who do not possess in themselves the divine and fruitful word." Wherefore, he says, "men of this kind are carried about both by winds and violent blasts." "Trees," he says, "of autumn, without fruit,"— unbelievers, that is, who bear no fruit of fidelity. "Twice dead," he says: once, namely, when they sinned by transgressing, and a second time when delivered up to punishment, according to the predestined judgments of God; inasmuch as it is to be reckoned death, even when each one does not forthwith deserve the inheritance. "Waves," he says, "of a raging sea." By these words he signifies the life of the Gentiles, whose end is abominable ambition. "Wandering stars,"—that is, he means those who err and are apostates are of that kind of stars which fell from the seats of the angels—"to whom," for their apostasy, "the blackness of darkness is reserved for ever. Enoch also, the seventh from Adam," he says, "prophesied of these." In these words he verities the prophecy.

"Those," he says, "separating" the faithful from the unfaithful, be convicted according to their own unbelief. And again those separating from the flesh. He says, "Animal not having the spirit;" that is, the spirit which is by faith, which supervenes through the practice of righteousness.

"But ye, beloved," he says, "building up yourselves on your most holy faith, in the Holy Spirit." "But some," he says, "save, plucking them from the fire;" "but of some have compassion in fear," that is, teach those who fall into the fire to free themselves. "Hating," he says, "that spotted garment, which is carnal:" that of the soul, namely; the spotted garment is a spirit polluternal lusts.

"Now to Him," he says, "who is able to keep you without stumbling, and present you faultless before the presence of His glory in joy." In the presence of His glory: he means in the presence of the angels, to be presented faultless, having become angels. When Daniel speaks of the people and comes into the presence of the Lord, he does not say this, because he saw God: for it is impossible that anyone whose heart is not pure should see God; but he says this, that everything that the people did was in the sight of God, and was manifest to Him; that is, that nothing is hid from the Lord.

Now, in the Gospel according to Mark, the Lord being interrogated by the chief of the priests if He was the Christ, the Son of the blessed God, answering, said, "I am; and ye shall see the Son of man sitting at the right hand of power." But powers mean the holy angels. Further, when He says "at the right hand of God," He means the self-same [beings], by reason of the equality and likeness of the angelic and holy powers, which are called by the name of God. He says, therefore, that He sits at the right hand; that is, that He rests in pre-eminent honor. In the other Gospels, however, He is said not to have replied to the high priest, on his asking if He was the Son of God. But what said He? "You say." Answering sufficiently well. For had He said, It is as you understand, he would have said what was not true, not confessing Himself to be the Son of God; [for] they did not entertain this opinion of Him; but by saying "You say," He spake truly. For what they had no knowledge of, but expressed in words, that he confessed to be true.

III.—COMMENTS ON THE FIRST EPISTLE OF JOHN.

Chap. i. 1. "That which was from the beginning; which we have seen with our eyes; which we have heard."

Following the Gospel according to John, and in accordance with it, this Epistle also contains the spiritual principle.

What therefore he says, "from the beginning," the Presbyter explained to this effect, that the beginning of generation is not separated from the beginning of the Creator. For when he says, "That which was from the beginning," he touches upon the generation without beginning of the Son, who is co-existent with the Father. There was; then, a Word importing an unbeginning eternity; as also the Word itself, that is, the Son of God, who being, by equality of substance, one with the Father, is eternal and uncreate. That He was always the Word, is signified by saying, "In the beginning was the Word." But by the expression, "we have seen with our eyes," he signifies the Lord's presence in the flesh, "and our hands have handled," he says, "of the Word of life." He means not only His flesh, but the virtues of the Son, like the sunbeam which penetrates to the lowest places,—this sunbeam coming in the flesh became palpable to the disciples. It is accordingly related in traditions, that John, touching the outward body itself, sent his hand deep down into it, and that the solidity of the flesh offered no obstacle, but gave way to the hand of the disciple.

"And our hands have handled of the Word of life;" that is, He who came in the flesh became capable of being touched. As also,

Ver. 2. "The life was manifested." For in the Gospel he thus speaks: "And what was made, in Him was life, and the life was the light of men."

"And we show unto you that eternal life, which was with the Father, and was manifested unto you."

He signifies by the appellation of Father, that the Son also existed always, without beginning.

Ver. 5. "For God," he says, "is light."

He does not express the divine essence, but wishing to declare the majesty of God, he has applied to the Divinity what is best and most excellent in the view of men. Thus also Paul, when he speaks of "light inaccessible." But John himself also in this same Epistle says, "God is love:" pointing out the excellences of God, that He is kind and merciful; and because He is light, makes men righteous, according to the advancement of the soul, through charity. God, then, who is ineffable in respect of His substance, is light.

"And in Him is no darkness at all,"—that is, no passion, no keeping up of evil respecting any one, [He] destroys no one, but gives salvation to all. Light moreover signifies, either the precepts of the Law, or faith, or doctrine. Darkness is the opposite of these things. Not as if there were another way; since there is only one way according to the divine precepts. For the work of God is unity. Duality and all else that exists, except unity, arises from perversity of life.

Ver. 7. "And the blood of Jesus Christ His Son," he says, "cleanses us." For the doctrine of the Lord, which is very powerful, is called His blood.

Ver. 10. "If we say that we have not sinned, we make Him a liar, and His word is not in us." His doctrine, that is, or word is truth.

Chap. ii. 1. "And if any man sin," he says, "we have an advocate with the Father, Jesus Christ." For so the Lord is an advocate with the Father for us. So also is there, an advocate, whom, after His assumption, He vouchsafed to send. For these primitive and first created virtues are unchangeable as to substance, and along with subordinate angels and archangels, whose names they share, effect divine operations. Thus also Moses names the virtue of the angel Michael, by an angel near to himself and of lowest grade. The like also we find in the holy prophets; but to Moses an angel appeared near and at hand. Moses heard him and spoke to him manifestly, face to face. On the other prophets, through the agency of angels, an impression was made, as of beings hearing and seeing.

On this account also, they alone heard, and they alone saw; as also is seen in the case of Samuel. Elisæus also alone heard the voice by which he was called. If the voice had been open and common, it would have been heard by all. In this instance it was heard by him alone in whom the impression made by the angel worked.

Ver. 2. "And not only for our sins,"—that is for those of the faithful,—is the Lord the propitiator, does he say, "but also for the whole world." He, indeed, saves all; but some [He saves], converting them by punishments; others, however, who follow voluntarily [He saves] with dignity of honor; so "that every knee should bow to Him, of things in heaven, and things on earth, and things under the earth;" that is, angels, men, and souls that before His advent have departed from this temporal life.

Ver. 3. "And by this we know that we know Him, if we keep His commandments." For the Gnostic [he who knows] also does the Works which pertain to the province of virtue. But he who performs the works is not necessarily also a Gnostic. For a man may be a doer of right works, and yet not a knower of the mysteries of science. Finally, knowing that some works are performed from fear of punishment, and some on account of the promise of reward, he shows the perfection of the man gifted with knowledge, who fulfils his works by love. Further, he adds, and says:—

Ver. 5. "But whoso keepeth His word, in him verily is the love of God perfected: hereby know we that we are in Him,"—by faith and love.

Ver. 7. "I write no new commandment unto you, but an old commandment, which ye had from the beginning,"—through the Law, that is, and the prophets; where it is said, God is one. Accordingly, also, he infers, "For the old commandment is the word which ye have heard."

Again, however, he says:—

Ver. 8. "This is the commandment; for the darkness" of perversion, that is, "has passed away, and, lo, the true light hath already shone,"—that is, through faith, through knowledge, through the Covenant working in men, through prepared judgments.

Ver. 9. "He that saith he is in the light,"—in the light, he means in the truth,—"and hateth," he says, "his brother." By his brother, he means not only his neighbor, but also the Lord. For unbelievers hate Him and do not keep His commandments. Therefore also he infers:—

Ver. 10. "He that loveth his brother abideth in the light; and there is none occasion of stumbling in him."

Vers. 12–14. He then indicates the stages of advancement and progress of souls that are still located in the flesh; and calls those whose sins have been forgiven, for the Lord's name's sake, "little children," for many believe on account of the name only. He styles "fathers" the perfect, "who have known what was from the beginning," and received with understanding,—the Son, that is, of whom he said above, "that which was from the beginning."

"I write," says he, "to you, young men, because ye have overcome the wicked one." Young man strong in despising pleasures. "The wicked one" points out the eminence of the devil. "The children," moreover, know the Father; having fled from idols and gathered together to the one God.

Ver. 15. "For the world," he says, "is in the wicked one." Is not the world, and all that is in the world, called God's creation and very good? Yes. But,

Ver. 16. "The lust of the flesh, the lust of the eyes, and the ambition of the world," which arise from the perversion of life, "are not of the Father, but of the world," and of you.

Ver. 17. "Therefore also the world shall pass away, and the lust thereof; but he that doeth the will of God" and His commandments "abideth for ever."

Ver. 19. "They went out from us; but they were not of us"—neither the apostate angels, nor men falling away;—"but that they may be manifested that they are not of us." With sufficient clearness he distinguishes the class of the elect and that of the lost, and that which remaining in faith "has an unction from the Holy One," which comes through faith. He that abideth not in faith.

Ver. 22. "A liar" and "an antichrist, who denieth that Jesus is the Christ." For Jesus, Savior and Redeemer, is also Christ the King.

Ver. 23. "He who denies the Son," by ignoring Him, "has not the Father, nor does he know Him." But he who knoweth the Son and the Father, knows according to knowledge, and when the Lord shall be manifested at His second advent, shall have confidence and not be confounded. Which confusion is heavy punishment.

Ver. 29. "Every one," he says, "who doeth righteousness is born of God;" being regenerated, that is, according to faith.

Chap. iii. 1. "For the world knoweth us not, as it knew Him not." He means by the world those who live a worldly life in pleasures.

Ver. 2. "Beloved," says he, "now are we the sons of God," not by natural affection, but because we have God as our Father. For it is the greater love that, seeing we have no relationship to God, He nevertheless loves us and calls us His sons. "And it hath not yet appeared what we shall be;" that is, to what kind of glory we shall attain. "For if He shall be manifested,"— that is, if we are made perfect,—"we shall be like Him," as reposing and justified, pure in virtue, "so that we may see Him" (His countenance) "as He is," by comprehension.

Ver. 8. "He that doeth unrighteousness is of the devil," that is, of the devil as his father, following and choosing the same things. "The devil sinneth from the beginning," he says. From the beginning from which he began to sin, incorrigibly persevering in sinning.

Ver. 9. He says, "Whosoever is born of God does not commit sin, for His seed remaineth in him;" that is, His word in him who is born again through faith.

Ver. 10. "Thus we know the children of God, as likewise the children of the devil," who choose things like the devil; for so also they are said to be of the wicked one.

Ver. 15. "Every one who hateth his brother is a murderer." For in him through unbelief Christ dies. Rightly, therefore, he continues, "And ye know that no murderer and unbeliever hath eternal life abiding in him." For the living Christ abides in the believing soul.

Ver. 16. "For He Himself laid down His life for us;" that is, for those who believe; that is, for the apostles. If then He laid down His life for the apostles, he means His apostles themselves: us if he said, We, I say, the apostles, for whom He laid down His life, "ought to lay down our lives for the brethren;" for the salvation of their neighbors was the glory of the apostles.

Ver. 20. He says, "For God is greater than our heart;" that is, the virtue of God [is greater] than conscience, which will follow the soul. Wherefore he continues, and says, "and knoweth all things."

Ver. 21. "Beloved, if our heart condemn us not, it will have confidence before God."

Ver. 24. "And hereby we know that He dwelleth in us by His Spirit, which He hath given us;" that is, by superintendence and foresight of future events.

Chap. iv. 18. He says, "Perfect love casteth out fear." For the perfection of a believing man is love.

Chap. v. 6. He says, "This is He who came by water and blood;" and again,—

Ver. 8. "For there are three that bear witness, the spirit," which is life, "and the water," which is regeneration and faith, "and the blood," which is knowledge; "and these three are one." For in the Savior are those saving virtues, and life itself exists in His own Son.

Ver. 14. "And this is the confidence which we have towards Him, that if we ask anything according to His will, He will hear us." He does not say absolutely what we shall ask, but what we ought to ask.

Ver. 19. "And the whole word lieth in the wicked one;" not the creation, but worldly men, and those who live according to their lusts.

Ver. 20. "And the Son of God hath come and given us understanding," which comes to us, that is, by faith, and is also called the Holy Spirit.

IV.—COMMENTS ON THE SECOND EPISTLE OF JOHN.

The second Epistle of John, which is written to Virgins, is very simple. It was written to a Babylonian lady, by name Electa, and indicates the election of the holy Church. He establishes in this Epistle that the following out of the faith is not without charity, and so that no one divide Jesus Christ; but only to believe that Jesus Christ has come in the flesh. For he who has the Son by apprehension in his intellect knows also the Father, and grasps with his mind intelligibly the greatness of His power working without beginning of time.

Ver. 10. He says, "If any come unto you and bring not this doctrine, receive him not into your house, neither bid him God speed; for he that biddeth him God speed is partaker of his evil deeds." He forbids us to salute such, and to receive them to our hospitality. For this is not harsh in the case of a man of this sort. But he admonishes them neither to confer nor dispute with such as are not able to handle divine things with intelligence, lest through them they be seduced from the doctrine of truth, influenced by plausible reasons. Now, I think that we are not even to pray with such, because in the prayer which is made at home, after rising from prayer, the salutation of joy is also the token of peace.

II.—NICETAS BISHOP OF HERACLEA.

FROM HIS CATENA.

I.—JOB I. 21.

But Job's words may be more elegantly understood of evil and sin thus: "Naked" was formed from the earth at the beginning, as if from a "mother's womb: naked to the earth shall I also depart;" naked, not of possessions, for that were a trivial and common thing, but of evil and sin, and of the unsightly shape which follows those who have led bad lives. Obviously, all of us human beings are born naked, and again are buried naked, swathed only in grave-clothes. For God hath provided for us another life, and made the present life the way for the course which leads to it; appointing the supplies derived from what we possess merely as provisions for the way; and on our quitting this way, the wealth, consisting of the things which we possessed, journeys no farther with us. For not a single thing that we possess is properly our own: of one possession alone, that is godliness, are we properly owners. Of this, death, when it overtakes us, will not rob us; but from all else it will eject us, though against our will. For it is for the support of life that we all have received what we possess; and after enjoying merely the use of it, each one departs, obtaining from life a brief remembrance. For this is the end of all prosperity; this is the conclusion of the good things of this life. Well, then, does the infant, on opening its eyes, after issuing from the womb, immediately begin with crying, not with laughter. For it weeps, as if bewailing life, at whose hands from the outset it tastes of deadly gifts. For immediately on being born its hands and feet are swaddled; and swathed in bonds it takes the breast. O introduction to life, precursor of death! The child has but just entered on life, and straightway there is put upon it the raiment of the dead: for nature reminds those that are born of their end. Wherefore also the child, on being born, wails, as if crying plaintively to its mother. Why, O mother, didst thou bring me forth to this life, in which prolongation of life is progress to death? Why hast thou brought me into this troubled world, in which, on being born, swaddling bands are my first experience? Why hast thou delivered me to such a life as this, in which both a pitiable youth wastes away before old age, and old age is shunned as under the doom of death? Dreadful, O mother, is the course of life, which has death as the goal of the runner. Bitter is the road of life we travel, with the grave as the wayfarer's inn. Perilous the sea of life we sail; for it has Hades as a pirate to attack us. Man alone is born in all respects naked, without a weapon or clothing born with him; not as being inferior to the other animals, but that nakedness and your bringing nothing with you may produce thought; and that thought may bring out dexterity, expel sloth, introduce the arts for the supply of our needs, and beget variety of contrivances. For, naked, man is full of contrivances, being pricked on by his necessity, as by a goad, how to escape rains, how to elude cold, how to fence off blows, how to till the earth, how to terrify wild beasts, how to subdue the more powerful of them. Wetted with rain, he contrived a roof; having suffered from cold, he invented clothing; being struck, he constructed a breastplate; bleeding his hands with the thorns in tilling the ground, he availed himself of the help of tools; in his naked state liable to become a prey to wild beasts, he discovered from his fear an art which frightened what frightened him. Nakedness begat one accomplishment after another; so that even his nakedness was a gift and a master-favor. Accordingly, Job also being made naked of wealth, possessions, of the blessing of children, of a numerous offspring, and having lost everything in a short time, uttered this grateful exclamation: "Naked came I out of the womb, naked also shall I depart thither;"—to God, that is, and to that blessed lot and rest.

II.—FROM THE SAME.

Job v. 7. Calmness is a thing which, of all other things, is most to be prized. As an example of this, the word proposes to us the blessed Job. For it is said of him, "What man is like Job, who drinketh up scorning like water?" For truly enviable, and, in my judgment, worthy of all admiration, a man is, if he has attained to such a degree of long-suffering as to be able with ease to grapple with the pain, truly keen, and not easily conquered by everybody, which arises from being wronged.

III.—FROM NICETAS' CATENA ON MATTHEW.

Matt. v. 42. Alms are to be given, but with judgment, and to the deserving, that we may obtain a recompense from the Most High. But woe to those who have and who take under false pretences, or who are able to help themselves and want to take from others. For he who has, and, to carry out false pretences or out of laziness, takes, shall be condemned.

IV.—FROM THE SAME.

Matt. xiii. 31. The word which proclaims the kingdom of heaven is sharp and pungent as mustard, and represses bile, that is, anger, and checks inflammation, that is, pride; and from this word the soul's true health and eternal soundness flow. To such increased size did the growth of the word come, that the tree which sprang from it (that is the Church of Christ established over the whole earth) filled the world, so that the fowls of the air—that is, divine angels and lofty souls—dwelt in its branches.

V.—FROM THE SAME.

Matt. xiii. 46. A pearl, and that pellucid and of purest ray, is Jesus, whom of the lightning flash of Divinity the Virgin bore. For as the pearl, produced in flesh and the oyster-shell and moisture, appears to be a body moist and transparent, full of light and spirit; so also God the Word, incarnate, is intellectual light, sending His rays, through a body luminous and moist.

III.—FROM THE CATENA ON LUKE, EDITED BY CORDERIUS.

Luke iii. 22. God here assumed the "likeness" not of a man, but "of a dove," because He wished, by a new apparition of the Spirit in the likeness of a dove, to declare His simplicity and majesty.

Luke xvi. 17. Perhaps by the iota and tittle His righteousness cries, "If ye come right unto Me, I will also come right to you; but if crooked, I also will come crooked, saith the Lord of hosts;" intimating that the ways of sinners are intricate and crooked. For the way right and agreeable to nature which is intimated by the iota of Jesus, is His goodness, which constantly directs those who believe from hearing. "There shall not, therefore, pass from the law one iota or one tittle," neither from the right and good the mutual promises, nor from the crooked and unjust the punishment assigned to them. "For the Lord doeth good to the good, but those who turn aside into crooked ways God will lead with the workers of iniquity."

IV.—FROM THE BOOKS OF THE HYPOTYPOSES. OECUMENIUS FROM BOOK III. ON 1 COR. XI. 10.

"Because of the angels." By the angels he means righteous and virtuous men. Let her be veiled then, that she may not lead them to stumble into fornication. For the real angels in heaven see her though veiled.

THE SAME, BOOK IV. ON 2 COR. V. 16.

"And if we have known Christ after the flesh." As "after the flesh" in our case is being in the midst of sins, and being out of them is "not after the flesh;" so also "after the flesh" in the case of Christ was His subjection to natural affections, and His not being subject to them is to be "not after the flesh." But, he says, as He was released, so also are we.

THE SAME, BOOK IV. ON 2 COR. VI. 11.

"Our heart is enlarged," to teach you all things. But ye are straitened in your own bowels, that is, in love to God, in which ye ought to love me.

THE SAME, BOOK V. ON GAL. V. 24.

"And they that are Christ's [have crucified] the flesh." And why mention one aspect of virtue after another? For there are some who have crucified themselves as far as the passions are concerned, and the passions as far as respects themselves. According to this interpretation the "and" is not superfluous. "And they that are Christ's"—that is, striving after Him—"have crucified their own flesh."

MOSCHUS: SPIRITUAL MEADOW, BOOK V. CHAP. 176.

Yes, truly, the apostles were baptized, as Clement the Stromatist relates in the fifth book of the Hypotyposes. For, in explaining the apostolic statement, "I thank God that I baptized none of you," he says, Christ is said to have baptized Peter alone, and Peter Andrew, and Andrew John, and they James and the rest.

EUSEBIUS: ECCLESIASTICAL HISTORY, BOOK VI. II. 1.

Now Clement, writing in the sixth book of the Hypotyposes, makes this statement. For he says that Peter and James and John, after the Savior's ascension, though preeminently honored by the Lord, did not contend for glory, but made James the Just, bishop of Jerusalem.

EUSEBIUS: ECCLESIASTICAL HISTORY, II. 15.

So, then, through the visit of the divine word to them, the power of Simon was extinguished, and immediately was destroyed along with the man himself. And such a ray of godliness shone forth on the minds of Peter's hearers, that they were not satisfied with the once hearing or with the unwritten teaching of the divine proclamation, but with all manner of entreaties importuned Mark, to whom the Gospel is ascribed, he being the companion of Peter, that he would leave in writing a record of the teaching which had been delivered to them verbally; and did not let the man alone till they prevailed upon him; and so to them we owe the Scripture called the "Gospel by Mark." On learning what had been done, through the revelation of the Spirit, it is said that the apostle was delighted with the enthusiasm of the men, and sanctioned the composition for reading in the Churches. Clemens gives the narrative in the sixth book of the Hypotyposes.

EUSEBIUS: IBID.

Then, also, as the divine Scripture says, Herod, on the execution of James, seeing that what was done pleased the Jews, laid hands also on Peter; and having put him in chains, would have presently put him to death, had not an angel in a divine vision appeared to him by night, and wondrously releasing him from his bonds, sent him away to the ministry of preaching.

EUSEBIUS: ECCLESIASTICAL HISTORY, VI. 14.

And in the Hypotyposes, in a word, he has made abbreviated narratives of the whole testamentary Scripture; and has not passed over the disputed books,—I mean Jude and the rest of the Catholic Epistles and Barnabas, and what is called the Revelation of Peter. And he says that the Epistle to the Hebrews is Paul's, and was written to the Hebrews in the Hebrew language; but that Luke, having carefully translated it, gave it to the Greeks, and hence the same coloring in the expression is discoverable in this Epistle and the Acts; and that the name "Paul an Apostle" was very properly not prefixed, for, he says, that writing to the Hebrews, who were prejudiced against him and suspected, he with great wisdom did not repel them in the beginning by putting down his name.

1 Tim. ii. 6. "In his times;" that is, when men were in a condition of fitness for faith.

1 Tim. iii. 16. "Was seen of angels." O mystery! The angels saw Christ while He was with us, not having seen Him before. Not as by men.

1 Tim. v. 8. "And especially those of his own house." He provides for his own and those of his own house, who not only provides for his relatives, but also for himself, by extirpating the passions.

1 Tim. v. 10. "If she have washed the feet of saints;" that is, if she has performed without shame the meanest offices for the saints.

1 Tim. v. 21. "Without prejudice;" that is, without falling under the doom and punishment of disobedience through making any false step.

1 Tim. vi. 13. "Who witnessed before Pontius Pilate." For He testified by what he did that He was Christ the Son of God.

2 Tim. ii. 2. "By many witnesses;" that is, the law and the prophets. For these the apostle made witnesses of his own preaching.

EUSEBIUS: ECCLESIASTICAL HISTORY, BOOK. VII. II. 1.

To James the Just, and John and Peter, the Lord after

His resurrection imparted knowledge (τὴν γνῶσιν.) These

imparted it to the rest of the apostles, and the rest of the apostles to the Seventy, of whom Barnabas was one.

EUSEBIUS: THE SAME, II. 2.

And of this James, Clement also relates an anecdote worthy of remembrance in the seventh book of the Hypotyposes, from a tradition of his predecessors. He says that the man who brought him to trial, on seeing him bear his testimony, was moved, and confessed that he was a Christian himself. Accordingly, he says, they were both led away together, and on the way the other asked James to forgive him. And he, considering a little, said, "Peace be to thee" and kissed him. And so both were beheaded together.

EUSEBIUS: THE SAME, VI. 14.

And now, as the blessed Presbyter used to say, since the Lord, as the Apostle of the Almighty, was sent to the Hebrews, Paul, as having been sent to the Gentiles, did not subscribe himself apostle of the Hebrews, out of modesty and reverence for the Lord, and because, being the herald and apostle of the Gentiles, his writing to the Hebrews was something over and above [his assigned function.]

EUSEBIUS: THE SAME.

Again, in the same books Clement has set down a tradition which he had received from the elders before him, in regard to the order of the Gospels, to the following effect. He says that the Gospels containing the genealogies were written first, and that the Gospel according to Mark was composed in the following circumstances:—

Peter having preached the word publicly at Rome, and by the Spirit proclaimed the Gospel, those who were present, who were numerous, entreated Mark, inasmuch as he had attended him from an early period, and remembered what had been said, to write down what had been spoken. On his composing the Gospel, he handed it to those who had made the request to him; which coming to Peter's knowledge, he neither hindered nor encouraged. But John, the last of all, seeing that what was corporeal was set forth in the Gospels, on the entreaty of his intimate friends, and inspired by the Spirit, composed a spiritual Gospel.

V.—FROM THE BOOK ON PROVIDENCE.

S. MAXIMUS, VOL. II. 114.

Being is in God. God is divine being, eternal and without beginning, incorporeal and illimitable, and the cause of what exists. Being is that which wholly subsists. Nature is the truth of things, or the inner reality of them. According to others, it is the production of what has come to existence; and according to others, again, it is the providence of God, causing the being, and the manner of being, in the things which are produced.

S. MAXIMUS: IN THE SAME, P. 152.

Willing is a natural power, which desires what is in accordance with nature. Willing is a natural appetency, corresponding with the nature of the rational creature. Willing is a natural spontaneous movement of the self-determining mind, or the mind voluntarily moved about anything. Spontaneity is the mind moved naturally, or an intellectual self-determining movement of the soul.

VI.—FROM THE BOOK ON THE SOUL.

MAXIMUS AND ANTONIUS MELISSA.

Souls that breathe free of all things, possess life, and though separated from the body, and found possessed of a longing for it, are borne immortal to the bosom of God: as in the winter season the vapors of the earth attracted by the sun's rays rise to him.

THE BAROCC. MS.

All souls are immortal, even those of the wicked, for whom it were better that they were not deathless. For, punished with the endless vengeance of quenchless fire, and not dying, it is impossible for them to have a period put to their misery.

VII.—FRAGMENT FROM THE BOOK ON SLANDER.

ANTONIUS MELISSA, BOOK. II. SERMON 69.

Never be afraid of the slanderer who addresses you. But rather say, Stop, brother; I daily commit more grievous errors, and how can I judge him? For you will gain two things, healing with one plaster both yourself and your neighbor. He shows what is really evil. Whence, by these arguments, God has contrived to make each one's disposition manifest.

ANTONIUS MELISSA, BOOK I. SERMON 64, AND BOOK II. SERMON 87. ALSO MAXIMUS, SERMON 59,P. 669; JOHN OF DAMASCUS, BOOK II.

It is not abstaining from deeds that justifies the believer, but purity and sincerity of thoughts.

VIII.—OTHER FRAGMENTS FROM ANTONIUS MELISSA.

I.—BOOK I. SERMON 17, ON CONFESSION.

Repentance then becomes capable of wiping out every sin, when on the occurrence of the soul's fault it admits no delay, and does not let the impulse pass on to a long space of time. For it is in this way that evil will be unable to leave a trace in us, being plucked away at the moment of its assault like a newly planted plant. As the creatures called crabs are easy to catch, from their going sometimes forward and sometimes backward; so also the soul, which at one time is laughing, at another weeping, and at another giving way to luxury, can do no good.

He who is sometimes grieving, and is sometimes enjoying himself and laughing, is like a man pelting the dog of voluptuousness with bread, who chases it in appearance, but in fact invites it to remain near him.

2. BOOK I. SERMON 51, ON PRAISE.

Some flatterers were congratulating a wise man. He said to them, If you stop praising me, I think myself something great after your departure; but if you do not stop praising me, I guess my own impurity. Feigned praise is worth less than true censure.

3. BOOK II. SERMON 46, ON THE LAZY AND INDOLENT.

To the weak and infirm, what is moderate appears excessive.

4. BOOK II. SERMON 55, ON YOUR NEIGHBOUR—THAT YOU ARE TO BEAR HIS BURDENS, ETC.

The reproof that is given with knowledge is very faithful. Sometimes also the knowledge of those who are condemned is found to be the most perfect demonstration.

5. BOOK II. SERMON 74, ON THE PROUD, AND THOSE DESIROUS OF VAINGLORY.

To the man who exalts and magnifies himself is attached the quick transition and the fall to low estate, as the divine word teaches.

6. BOOK II. SERMON 87.

Pure speech and a spotless life are the throne and true temple of God.

IX.—FRAGMENT OF THE TREATISE ON MARRIAGE. MAXIMUS,

SERMON III. P. 538, ON MODESTY AND CHASTITY. ALSO, JOHN OF DAMASCUS, BOOK III.—PARALLEL CHAP. 27.

It is not only fornication, but also the giving in marriage prematurely, that is called fornication; when, so to speak, one not of ripe age is given to a husband, either of her own accord or by her parents.

X.—FRAGMENTS OF OTHER LOST BOOKS.

MAXIMUS, SERMON 2.—JOHN OF DAMASCUS, II. CHAP. 70.—ANTONIUS MELISSA, BOOK I. SERMON 52.

Flattery is the bane of friendship. Most men are accustomed to pay court to the good fortune of princes, rather than to the princes themselves.

MAXIMUS, SERMON 13, P. 574.—ANTONIUS MELISSA, SERMON 32, P. 45, AND SERMON 33, P. 57.

The lovers of frugality shun luxury as the bane of soul and body. The possession and use of necessaries has nothing injurious in quality, but it has in quantity above measure. Scarcity of food is a necessary benefit.

MAXIMUS, SERMON 52, P. 654.—ANTONIUS MELISSA, BOOK I. SERMON 54.

The vivid remembrance of death is a check upon diet; and when the diet is lessened, the passions are diminished along with it.

MAXIMUS, SERMON 55, P. 661.

Above all, Christians are not allowed to correct with violence the delinquencies of sins. For it is not those that abstain from wickedness from compulsion, but those that abstain from choice, that God crowns. It is impossible for a man to be steadily good except by his own choice. For he that is made good by compulsion of another is not good; for he is not what he is by his own choice. For it is the freedom of each one that makes true goodness and reveals real wickedness. Whence through these dispositions God contrived to make His own disposition manifest.

XI.—FRAGMENTS FOUND IN GREEK ONLY IN THE OXFORD EDITION.
FROM THE LAST WORK ON THE PASSOVER. (QUOTED IN THE
PASCHAL CHRONICLE.)

Accordingly, in the years gone by, Jesus went to eat the Passover sacrificed by the Jews, keeping the feast. But when he had preached He who was the Passover, the Lamb of God, led as a sheep to the slaughter, presently taught His disciples the mystery of the type on the thirteenth day, on which also they inquired, "Where wilt Thou that we prepare for Thee to eat the Passover?" It was on this day, then, that both the consecration of the unleavened bread and the preparation for the feast took place. Whence John naturally describes the disciples as already previously prepared to have their feet washed by the Lord. And on the following day our Savior suffered, He who was the Passover, propitiously sacrificed by the Jews.

THE SAME.

Suitably, therefore, to the fourteenth day, on which He also suffered, in the morning, the chief priests and the scribes, who brought Him to Pilate, did not enter the Prætorium, that they might not be defiled, but might freely eat the Passover in the evening. With this precise determination of the days both the whole Scriptures agree, and the Gospels harmonize. The resurrection also attests it. He certainly rose on the third day, which fell on the first day of the weeks of harvest, on which the law prescribed that the priest should offer up the sheaf.

MACARIUS CHRYSOCEPHALUS: PARABLE OF THE PRODIGAL SON,
LUKE XV., ORATION ON LUKE XV., TOWARDS THE CLOSE.

1. What choral dance and high festival is held in heaven, if there is one that has become an exile and a fugitive from the life led under the Father, knowing not that those who put themselves far from Him shall perish; if he has squandered the gift, and substance, and inheritance of the Father; if there is one whose faith has failed, and whose hope is spent, by rushing along with the Gentiles into the same profligacy of debauchery; and then, famished and destitute, and not even filled with what the swine eat, has arisen and come to his Father!

But the kind Father waits not till the son comes to Him. For perchance he would never be able or venture to approach, did he not find Him gracious. Wherefore, when he merely wishing, when he straightway made a beginning, when he took the first step, while he was yet a great way off, He [the Father] was moved with compassion, and ran, and fell upon his neck and kissed him. And then the son, taking courage, confessed what he had done.

Wherefore the Father bestows on him the glory and honor that was due and meet, putting on him the best robe, the robe of immortality; and a ring, a royal signet and divine seal,—impress of consecration, signature of glory, pledge of testimony (for it is said, "He hath set to his seal that God is true,") and shoes, not those perishable ones which he hath set his foot on holy ground is bidden take off, nor such as he who is sent to preach the kingdom of heaven is forbidden to put on, but such as wear not, and are suited for the journey to heaven, becoming and adorning the heavenly path, such as unwashed feet never put on, but those which are washed by our Teacher and Lord.

Many, truly, are the shoes of the sinful soul, by which it is bound and cramped. For each man is cramped by the cords of his own sins. Accordingly, Abraham swears to the king of Sodom, "I will not take of all that is thine, from a thread to a shoe-latchet." On account of these being defiled and polluted on the earth, every kind of wrong and selfishness engrosses life. As the Lord reproves Israel by Amos, saying, "For three iniquities of Israel, yea, for four, I will not turn him back; because they have given away the righteous for silver, and the needy for a pair of shoes, which tread upon the dust of the ground."

2. Now the shoes which the Father bids the servant give to the repentant son who has betaken himself to Him, do not impede or drag to the earth (for the earthly tabernacle weighs down the anxious mind); but they are buoyant, and ascending, and waft to heaven, and serve as such a ladder and chariot as he requires who has turned his mind towards the Father. For, beautiful after being first beautifully adorned with all these things without, he enters into the gladness within. For "Bring out" was said by Him who had first said, "While he was yet a great way off, he ran and fell upon his neck." For it is here that all the preparation for entrance to the marriage to which we are invited must be accomplished. He, then, who has been made ready to enter will say, "This my joy is fulfilled." But the unlovely and unsightly man will hear, "Friend, how camest thou in here, without having a wedding garment?" And the fat and unctuous food,—the delicacies abundant and sufficing of the blessed,—the fatted calf is killed; which is also again spoken of as a lamb (not literally); that no one may suppose it small; but it is the great and greatest. For not small is "the Lamb of God who taketh away the sin of the world," who "was led as a sheep to the slaughter," the sacrifice full of marrow, all whose fat, according to the sacred law, was the Lord's. For He was wholly devoted and consecrated to the Lord; so well grown, and to such excessive size, as to reach and extend over all, and to fill those who eat Him and feed upon Him. For He is both flesh and bread, and has given Himself as both to us to be eaten.

To the sons, then, who come to Him, the Father gives the calf, and it is slain and eaten. But those who do not come to Him He pursues and disinherits, and is found to be a most powerful bull. Here, by reason of His size and prowess, it is said of Him, "His glory is as that of an unicorn." And the prophet Habakkuk sees Him bearing horns, and celebrates His defensive attitude—"horns in His hands." Wherefore the sign shows His power and authority,—horns that pierce on both sides, or rather, on all sides, and through everything. And those who eat are so strengthened, and retain such strength from the life-giving food in them, that they themselves are stronger than their enemies, and are all but armed with the horns of a bull; as it is said, "In thee shall we butt our enemies."

3. Gladness there is, and music, and dances; although the elder son, who had ever been with and ever obedient to the Father, takes it ill, when he who never had himself been dissipated or profligate sees the guilty one made happy.

Accordingly the Father calls him, saying, "Son, thou art ever with me." And what greater joy and feast and festivity can be than being continually with God, standing by His side and serving Him? "And all that is mine is thine." And blessed is the heir of God, for whom the Father holds possession,—the faithful, to whom the whole world of possessions belongs.

"It was meet that we should be glad, and rejoice; for thy brother was dead, and is alive again." Kind Father, who givest all things life, and raisest the dead. "And was lost, and is found." And "blessed is the man whom Thou hast chosen and accepted," and whom having sought, Thou dost find. "Blessed are those whose iniquities are forgiven, whose sins are covered." It is for man to repent of sins; but let this be accompanied with a change that will not be checked. For he who does not act so shall be put to shame, because he has acted not with his whole heart, but in haste.

And it is ours to flee to God. And let us endeavor after this ceaselessly and energetically. For He says, "Come unto Me, all ye that labor and are heavy laden, and I will give you rest." And prayer and confession with humility are voluntary acts. Wherefore it is enjoined, "First tell thy sins, that thou mayest be justified." What afterwards we shall obtain, and what we shall be, it is not for us to judge.

4. Such is the strict meaning of the parable. The repentant son came to the pitying Father, never hoping for these things,—the best robe, and the ring, and the shoes,—or to taste the fatted calf, or to share in gladness, or enjoy music and dances; but he would have been contented with obtaining what in his own estimation he deemed himself worth. "Make me," he had made up his mind to say, "as one of thy hired servants." But when he saw the Father's welcome meeting him, he did not say this, but said what he had in his mind to say first, "Father, I have sinned against Heaven, and before thee." And so both his humility and his accusation became the cause of justification and glory. For the righteous man condemns himself in his first words. So also the publican departed justified rather than the Pharisee. The son, then, knew not either what he was to obtain, or how to take or use or put on himself the things given him; since he did not take the robe himself, and put it on. But it is said, "Put it on him." He did not himself put the ring on his finger, but those who were bidden "Put a ring on his hand." Nor did he put the shoes on himself, but it was they who heard, "and shoes on his feet."

And these things were perhaps incredible to him and to others, and unexpected before they took place; but gladly received and praised were the gifts with which he was presented.

5. The parable exhibits this thought, that the exercise of the faculty of reason has been accorded to each man. Wherefore the prodigal is introduced, demanding from his father his portion, that is, of the state of mind, endowed by reason. For the possession of reason is granted to all, in order to the pursuit of what is good, and the avoidance of what is bad. But many who are furnished by God with this make a bad use of the knowledge that has been given them, and land in the profligacy of evil practices, and wickedly waste the substance of reason,—the eye on disgraceful sights, the tongue on

blasphemous words, the smell on foetid licentious excesses of pleasures, the mouth on swinish gluttony, the hands on thefts, the feet on running into plots, the thoughts on impious counsels, the inclinations on indulgence on the love of ease, the mind on brutish pastime. They preserve nothing of the substance of reason unsquandered. Such an one, therefore, Christ represents in the parable,—as a rational creature, with his reason darkened, and asking from the Divine Being what is suitable to reason; then as obtaining from God, and making a wicked use of what had been given, and especially of the benefits of baptism, which had been vouchsafed to him; whence also He calls him a prodigal; and then, after the dissipation of what had been given him, and again his restoration by repentance, [He represents] the love of God shown to him.

6. For He says, "Bring hither the fatted calf, kill it, and let us eat and be merry; for this my son"—a name of nearest relationship, and significative of what is given to the faithful— "was dead and lost,"—an expression of extremest alienation; for what is more alien to the living than the lost and dead? For neither can be possessed any more. But having from the nearest relationship fallen to extremest alienation, again by repentance he returned to near relationship. For it is said, "Put on him the best robe," which was his the moment he obtained baptism. I mean the glory of baptism, the remission of sins, and the communication of the other blessings, which he obtained immediately he had touched the font.

"And put a ring on his hand." Here is the mystery of the Trinity; which is the seal impressed on those who believe.

"And put shoes on his feet," for "the preparation of the Gospel of peace," and the whole course that leads to good actions.

7. But whom Christ finds lost, after sin committed since baptism, those Novatus, enemy of God, resigns to destruction. Do not let us then reckon any fault if we repent; guarding against falling, let us, if we have fallen, retrace our

steps. And while dreading to offend, let us, after offending, avoid despair, and be eager to be confirmed; and on sinking, let us haste to rise up again. Let us obey the Lord, who calls to us, "Come unto Me, all ye that labor, and I will give you rest." Let us employ the gift of reason for actions of prudence. Let us learn now abstinence from what is wicked, that we may not be forced to learn in the future. Let us employ life as a training school for what is good; and let us be roused to the hatred of sin. Let us bear about a deep love for the Creator; let us cleave to Him with our whole heart; let us not wickedly waste the substance of reason, like the prodigal. Let us obtain the joy laid up, in which Paul exulting, exclaimed, "Who shall separate us from the love of Christ?" To Him belongs glory and honor, with the Father and the Holy Spirit, world without end. Amen.

MACARIUS CHRYSOCEPHALUS: ORATION VIII. ON MATT. VIII., AND BOOK VII. ON LUKE XIII.

Therefore God does not here take the semblance of man, but of a dove, because He wished to show the simplicity and gentleness of the new manifestation of the Spirit by the likeness of the dove. For the law was stern, and punished with the sword; but grace is joyous, and trains by the word of meekness. Hence the Lord also says to the apostles, who said that He should punish with fire those who would not receive Him, after the manner of Elias: "Ye know not what manner of spirit ye are of."

FROM THE SAME.—BOOK XIII. CHAP. IX.

Possibly by the "iota and the tittle" His righteousness exclaims, "If ye come right to me, I also will come right to you; if ye walk crooked, I also will walk crooked, saith the Lord of hosts," alluding to the offences of sinners under the name of crooked ways. For the straightway, and that according to nature, which is pointed out by the iota of Jesus, is His goodness, which is immoveable towards those who have obediently believed. There shall not then pass away from the law neither the iota nor the tittle; that is, neither the promise that applies to the straight in the way, nor the punishment threatened against those that diverge. For the Lord is good to the straight in the way; but "those that turn aside after their crooked ways He shall lead forth with those that work iniquity." "And with the innocent He is innocent, and with the froward He is froward;" and to the crooked He sends crooked ways.

His own luminous image God impressed as with a seal, even the greatest,—on man made in His likeness, that he might be ruler and lord over all things, and that all things might serve him. Wherefore God judges man to be wholly His, and His own image. He is invisible; but His image, man, is visible. Whatever one, then, does to man, whether good or bad, is referred to Himself. Wherefore from Him judgment shall proceed, appointing to all according to desert; for He will avenge His own image.

XII.—FRAGMENTS NOT GIVEN IN THE OXFORD EDITION.
1.   IN ANASTASIUS SINAITA, QUEST. 96.

As it is possible even now for man to form men, according to the original formation of Adam, He no longer now creates, on account of His having granted once for all to man the power of generating men, saying to our nature, "Increase, and multiply, and replenish the earth." So also, by His omnipotent and omniscient power, He arranged that the dissolution and death of our bodies should be effected by a natural sequence and order, through the change of their elements, in accordance with His divine knowledge and comprehension.

2. JOANNES VECCUS, PATRIARCH OF CONSTANTINOPLE, ON THE PROCESSION OF THE SPIRIT. IN LEO ALLATIUS, VOL. I. P. 248.

Further, Clement the Stromatist, in the various definitions which he framed, that they might guide the man desirous of studying theology in every dogma of religion, defining what spirit is, and how it is called spirit, says: "Spirit is a substance, subtle, immaterial, and which issues forth without form."

3. FROM THE UNPUBLISHED DISPUTATION AGAINST ICONOCLASTS, OF NICEPHORUS OF CONSTANTINOPLE; EDITED IN GREEK AND LATIN BY LE NOURRY IN HIS APPARATUS TO THE LIBRARY OF THE FATHERS, VOL. I. P. 1334 A.B. FROM CLEMENT THE PRESBYTER OF ALEXANDRIA'S BOOK AGAINST JUDAIZERS.

Solomon the son of David, in the books styled "The Reigns of the Kings," comprehending not only that the structure of the true temple was celestial and spiritual, but had also a reference to the flesh, which He who was both the son and Lord of David was to build up, both for His own presence, where, as a living image, He resolved to make His shrine, and for the church that was to rise up through the union of faith, says expressly, "Will God in very deed dwell with men on the earth?"

He dwells on the earth clothed in flesh, and His abode with men is effected by the conjunction and harmony which obtains among the righteous, and which build and rear a new temple. For the righteous are the earth, being still encompassed with the earth; and earth, too, in comparison with the greatness of the Lord. Thus also the blessed Peter hesitates not to say, "Ye also, as living stones, are built up, a spiritual house, a holy temple, to offer up spiritual sacrifices, acceptable to God by Jesus Christ."

And with reference to the body, which by circumscription He consecrated as a hallowed place for Himself upon earth, He said, "Destroy this temple, and in three days I will raise it up again. The Jews therefore said, In forty-six years was this temple built, and wilt thou raise it up in three days? But He spake of the temple of His body."

4. FROM MS. MARKED 2431 IN THE LIBRARY OF THE MOST CHRISTIAN KING.—IBID. P. 1336 A. FROM THE VERY HOLY AND BLESSED CLEMENT, PRESBYTER OF ALEXANDRIA, THE STROMATIST'S BOOK ON PROVIDENCE.

What is God? "God," as the Lord saith, "is a Spirit." Now spirit is properly substance, incorporeal, and uncircumscribed. And that is incorporeal which does not consist of a body, or whose existence is not according to breadth, length, and depth. And that is uncircumscribed which has no place, which is wholly in all, and in each entire, and the same in itself.

5. FROM THE SAME MS.—IBID. 1335 D.

Φύσις (nature) is so called from τὸ πεφυκέναι (to be born). The first substance is everything which subsists by itself, as a stone is called a substance. The second is a substance capable of increase, as a plant grows and decays. The third is animated and sentient substance, as animal, horse. The fourth is animate, sentient, rational substance, as man. Wherefore each one of us is made as consisting of all, having an immaterial soul and a mind, which is the image of God.

6. IN JOHN OF DAMASCUS—PARALLEL—VOL. II. P. 307.

The fear of God, who is impassible, is free of perturbation. For it is not God that one dreads, but the falling away from God. He who dreads this, dreads falling into what is evil, and dreads what is evil. And he that fears a fall wishes himself to be immortal and passionless.

7. THE SAME, P. 341.

Let there be a law against those who dare to look at things sacred and divine irreverently, and in a way unworthy of God, to inflict on them the punishment of blindness.

8. THE SAME, P. 657.

Universally, the Christian is friendly to solitude, and quiet, and tranquility, and peace.

9. FROM THE CATENA ON THE PENTATEUCH, PUBLISHED IN LATIN BY FRANCIS ZEPHYRUS, P. 146.

That mystic name which is called the Tetragrammaton, by which alone they who had access to the Holy of Holies were protected, is pronounced Jehovah, which means, "Who is, and who shall be." The candlestick which stood at the south of the altar signified the seven planets, which seem to us to revolve around the meridian, on either side of which rise three branches; since the sun also like the lamp, balanced in the midst of the planets by divine wisdom, illumines by its light those above and below. On the other side of the altar was situated the table on which the loaves were displayed, because from that quarter of the heaven vital and nourishing breezes blow.

10. FROM J. A. CRAMER'S CATENÆ GRÆCORUM PATRUM IN NOV. TEST. OXFORD 1840 VOL. III.

On Acts vii. 24. The mystics say that it was by his word alone that Moses slew the Egyptian; as certainly afterwards it is related in the Acts that [Peter] slew with his word those who kept back part of the price of the land, and lied.

II. THE SAME, VOL. IV. P. 291.

On Rom. viii. 38. "Or life, that of our present existence," and "death,"—that caused by the assault of persecutors, and "angels, and principalities, and powers," apostate spirits.

12. P. 369, CHAP. X. 3.

And having neither known nor done the requirement of the law, what they conceived, that they also thought that the law required. And they did not believe the law, as prophesying, but the bare word; and followed it from fear, but not with their disposition and in faith.

13. VOL. VI. P. 385.

On 2 Cor. v. 16. "And if we have known Christ after the flesh."

And so far, he says, no one any longer lives after the flesh. For that is not life, but death. For Christ also, that He might show this, ceased to live after the flesh. How? Not by putting off the body! Far be it! For with it as His own He shall come, the Judge of all. But by divesting Himself of physical affections, such as hunger, and thirst, and sleep, and weariness. For now He has a body incapable of suffering and of injury.

As "after the flesh" in our case is being in the midst of sins, and being out of them is to be "not after the flesh;" so also after the flesh, in the case of Christ, was His subjection to natural affections, and not to be subject to them was not to be "after the flesh." "But," he says, "as He was released, so also are we." Let there be no longer, he says, subjection to the influences of the flesh. Thus Clement, the fourth book of the *Hypotyposes.*

14. FROM THE SAME, P. 391.

On 2 Cor. vi. 11. "Our heart is enlarged."

For as heat is wont to expand, so also love. For love is a thing of warmth. As if he would say, I love you not only with mouth, but with heart, and have you all within. Wherefore he says: "ye are not straitened in us, since desire itself expands the soul." "Our heart is enlarged" to teach you all things; "but ye are straitened in your own bowels," that is, in love to God, in which you ought to love me.

Thus Clement, in the fourth book of the *Hypotyposes*.

15. FROM VOL. III. V. 286.

Heb. i. 1. "At sundry times and divers manners."

Since the Lord, being the Apostle of the Almighty, was sent to the Hebrews, it was out of modesty that Paul did not subscribe himself apostle of the Hebrews, from reverence for the Lord, and because he was the herald and apostle of the Gentiles, and wrote the Epistle to the Hebrews in addition [to his proper work].

16. FROM THE SAME.

The same work contains a passage from *The Instructor*, book i. chap. vi. The passage is that beginning, "For the blood is found to be," down to "potent charms of affection." Portions, however, are omitted. There are a good many various readings; but although the passage in question, as found in Cramer's work, is printed in full in Migne's edition, on the alleged ground of the considerable variation from the text of Clement, the variation is not such as to make a translation of the passage as found in Cramer of any special interest or value.

We have noted the following readings:—

γινεται, where, the verb being omitted, we have inserted *is*: There is an obstruction, etc.

σύριγγας, tubes, instead of σήραγγας (hollows),

hollows of the breasts.

γειτνιαζουσῶν, for γειτνιουσῶν, neighboring

(arteries).

ἐπιλήψει, for ἐμπεριλήψει, interruption (such as this).

ἀποκλήρωσις occurs as in the text, for which the

emendation ἀπολήρησις, as specified

in the note, has been adopted.

ἥτις ἐστί, omitted here, which is "sweet through

grace," is supplied.

P. 142.

γάλα, milk, instead of μάννα, manna, (that food) manna.

P. 143.

χρὴ δὲ κατανοῆσαι τὴν φύσιν (but it is necessary to

consider nature), for οὐ κατανενοηκότες, τ. φ., through want of

consideration of nature.

κατακλειομένῳ, agreeing with food, for

κατακλειομένῳ, agreeing with heat (enclosed within).

γίνεται for γὰρ (which is untranslated), (the blood) is (a

preparation) for milk.

P. 144.

τοίνυν τὸν λόγον is supplied, and εἰκότως omitted in

the clause, Paul using appropriate figurative language.

P. 145.

πλὴ ν is supplied before ἀλλὰ τὸ ἐν αὐτῇ, and the

blood in it, etc., is omitted.

P. 146.

"For Diogenes Apolloniates will have it" is omitted.

πάντῃ, rendered "in all respects," is connected with the

preceding sentence.

P. 147.

ὅτι τοίνυν, for Ὡς δ'. And that (milk is produced).

τηνικαῦτα for τηνικάδε in the clause, "and the grass and

meadows are juicy and moist," not translated.

προειρημένῳ, above mentioned (milk), omitted.

τρυφῆς for τροφῆς, (sweet) nutriment.

τῷ omitted before γλυκεῖ, sweet (wine), and καθάπερ,

"as, when suffering."

τὸ λιπαρόν for τῷ λιπαρῷ, and ἀριδήλως for

ἀριδήλου, in the sentence: "Further, many use the fat of milk,

called butter, for the lamp, plainly," etc.

N. B.

[Le Nourry decides that the *Adumbrations* were not translated from the *Hypotyposes,* but Kaye (p. 473) thinks on insufficient grounds. See, also (p. 5), Kaye's learned note.]

Printed in Great Britain
by Amazon

85663180R00037